OUR COMMON GOAL
THAT UNITES THE WORLD

The Missing Piece
in the Jigsaw Puzzle of Life

LIBBY ROUSE

BORDERLANDS PRESS

Baltimore ❏ 1992

Our Common Goal That Unites The World
First Edition
Copyright © 1992 by Libby Rouse

Library of Congress Cataloging In Publication Data

Rouse, Libby
Our common goal that unites the world
Social ethics
LC Classifaction # HM 216
dc. 304.23
Library of Congress Catalog Card # 92-72152
ISBN# 1-880325-01-2

Back Cover Art by Portia Askew
Jacket & Book Design and Typesetting by Thomas F. Monteleone

Printed in the United States of America
Borderlands Press, P.O. Box 32333, Baltimore MD 21208
For information on ordering additional copies of this title either retail or wholesale, call (800)528-3310

Dedication

To anyone who cares to read this,
but especially to my beloved children
and grandchildren

. . . . a legacy . . . .

May your motives stay pure
and your lives follow
your own insights of Love

May our Common Goal synthesize and integrate
for you all of your living,
as it has for me . . .

To Fear Love
is to fear life . . .

—Bertrand Russell

CONTENTS

FOREWORD

I want to say two things to my readers:

1. ***Synthesis is my goal.*** There are many, many fine books and programs available in the areas of World-Views and Human Relationships. I therefore hope my contribution will be to set forth in a single, unified and cohesive manner what I see as a universal integration of them all. I hope to clear a little the confusing mists of daily living and dealing with our fellow travelers, by offering a reasonable and usable guide, one which will help us moment by moment to better see our way.

2. It is my hope that having initiated a non-profit organization called "Centers for Human Understanding" that this writing will serve not only as a legacy within my family, but as background thinking for the Center's current notion of developing a World's Fair type "**Pavilion of Life**". . . The hope of the Pavilion is to inspire . . . not only an uplifting, universal, planetary world-view . . . but to teach experientially through "hands-on" monitors, the newly emerging Conflict Resolution Process.

Note: It is difficult to cope with the "he/she" language issues . . . When our feminists coin better words than are provided by the broad use of "man," "brotherhood," etc., I am eager to use those new words.. Know that for now, whatever gender words I use, I am equally for all people, both male and female, and that I will do my best to unisex my words. You can count on the fact I care as deeply that women be respected for their unique role and rights, as that men be respected for theirs.

CHAPTER 1

The Mess We're In . . .
The Condition Of Man

    Problems! Problems! Problems! We are all used to the long enumerations of problems we face in the world today, problems which the newspapers, newscasts, and talk shows throw at us daily. Because of this outpouring, we become nearly immune to the issues, feeling helpless and lost as to what to do. We find that even our world leaders seem lost . . . If we try to list the problems of this country, they run something like this:

We have an exceedingly high rate of divorce;
There is a high rate of child abuse,
Youth Abuse,
Drug Abuse,
Teenage pregnancy,
A. I. D. S.,
Violence,
Murders,
Joblessness,
Poverty,
An unmanageable economy,
A polluted environment,
Miserably fractured lives,
and Personal isolation!

Even the families that are together are dysfunctional. I heard John Bradshaw recently say on TV that Virginia Satir, a well known therapist, had stated that 96% of our families were dysfunctional, and Bradshaw, also a therapist, replied: "No, you are wrong. They are all dysfunctional to some degree."

We hear too, of the problems of the elderly and the homeless. Real and vital Family Clans or Communities *in* the cities are lacking, or meaningless. Cities are mostly constructed of solid concrete and high-rise solidarity—no trees, no *immediate* connection with Nature. Without a connection to Nature, our young miss out on a sense of awe, and wonder, and meaningfulness. There is no question that the Design of Cities helps or hinders all of our problems, and there is no question that the Societal Systems within the cities help or hinder them. Most of our cities are obsolete. They just don't work with the kind of non-design and overwhelmed systems that now exist.

Most schools are ineffective. They are much too large and cannot respond to students' developmental needs. The cities themselves are also much too large. People feel lost and as though they haven't any say in their government. The economy seems out of hand. We have a huge national debt, the interest on which is using up money needed for social aims. Great masses of people are living in poverty and joblessness . . .

There are two approaches to these problems:
— one is rescue,
— the other is prevention.

For those people who are social workers, nurses, doctors, and just everyday people volunteering their time to help with these kinds of problems, I have the greatest admiration and gratitude. They are the ones I call *rescuers*. But there is also the need to work at the *prevention* of these problems. I love the old quip: "What's the sense of mopping up the floor if we don't turn off the faucet?"

In order to get into prevention, however, we need to take a look at the Parts and Pieces of this mess we're in, this Jig-saw-Puzzle-of-Life, to see if understanding them and what we are up against will guide us to intelligent solutions. We need solutions that deal with the whole spectrum of these Parts and Pieces, rather than solutions that deal just with the Parts and Pieces themselves. Both approaches are essential. Both rescue roles and prevention programs are essential, but in today's world, we primarily have rescue programs.

As I see it, this Jig-saw-puzzle of life is made up of Players, as well as Parts and Pieces. If we were to make a list with the Players on one side and the Pieces on the other, the puzzle would look something like this:

The Players — The "Who"

The Players are people with differing World Views and Motivation, whether they are conscious of their World View and Motivation or not.

The Players have been given gifts and tasks that help or hinder them as they go about their Journey of Living.

The Players are at different points of maturity and wisdom on this all important Journey of Life

The Players speak different languages and few know well how to communicate, even within the same language.[1]

The Pieces — The Life Style Patterns and Systems

Nuclear family groups of 2, 3, 4, or more

Family Clan groups, including Singles

The Communities and environments we live in:

their Design,
their Systems of

Government
Economics
Education

[1]Some players are operating under special conditions of war, disaster, or poverty, and require special attention.

As I said before, thank God for those hundreds and hundreds of people out there, who, in their jobs and volunteer work do the rescuing that is needed . . . the rescue work resulting from the malfunctions of the Players and Pieces in our society. As suggested, we must come up with another approach to these problems. one that will constitute the prevention of them. "Where there is no vision the people perish."

So, what can we do with such a Jig-saw Puzzle? How should we view it and how can we put all these Players and Pieces together in such a way that they are developmental of health and joy instead of misery and pain? How can we prevent or at least lessen "The Mess We're In?"

CHAPTER 2

Our Common Goal
That Unites The World

    The way we can begin to put it all together is to recognize the need for a uniting goal. For years in this country we have honored and espoused diversity and this is an important precept to hang on to, but we've neglected to search for and espouse any kind of clear uniting goal. We need a new "oneness-of-mind." In our past and even our present we are somewhat like the Headless Horseman riding off in all directions . . .

    Is there such a goal? Could there possibly be a goal that would be acceptable to everyone, and unite us? Yes, I believe there is. It is "a given," already there for us. We have all been given a Common Goal; namely, each of us deep down, wants:

TO LOVE, BE LOVED AND BE PRODUCTIVE.

This is our given. It is our common, universal goal. All religions, therapists, humanists, do-gooders, attest to this goal. When we get down to the bottom of all the hates and encrustations of bad habits that people get themselves into, or fall into, or are unwittingly forced as children into, this is the most basic and deepest desire all people seem to have. So let's grab onto it, accept it as our Common Goal, and see what such an acceptance will do for us. Recognition of, awareness of, this unifying, universal, Common Goal just may be the *Missing Piece* in the Jigsaw-Puzzle of Life.

First though, there are so many different definitions of Love in the world, we need to define what we mean by Love. Voltaire wrote "Before you talk with me, define your terms." In all my explorations, searching for how others in history, or today, have defined Love, I have discovered the following: many of our historic leaders, religious, psychiatric, psychological, sociological, literary, poetic, have talked about love.

Alfred Adler said, "There is a law that man should love his neighbor as himself. In a few hundred years this should be as natural to mankind, as healthy as the upright gait, but if man does not learn it, he must perish."

Benjamin Disraeli said, "We are all born for love; it is the principal of existence, and its only end."

One of my favorites, because it is so fundamental and incisive, is St. Augustine's "Love God and do as you please."

St. Bonaventure said, "Any old woman can love God better than a Doctor of Theology."

George Granville in "Pelius and Thetis" said, "There is no heaven like mutual love."

All these observations give us insights into love, but none really tells us what love *is,* what constitutes *healthy* love. Someone asked Jesus of Nazareth to sum up the commandments, and He answered with the well known:

"Love the Lord thy God with all thy heart, with all thy soul (spirit), with all thy mind, and love thy neighbor as thyself."

He also called us to a "Brotherhood of Love" through which He commanded us to find a way to include *all* human kind in a loving circle, keeping a feeling of Love going in whatever we were doing. So from Jesus, *who was not a Christian, but a man for All Others, a Universal Man,* we learn that Love is made of 4-Loves: Love of God, Love of Self, Love of Other, and Love of All. So if love is 4-Loves, let us next look, in broad scope, at what we mean by each of these Loves.

LOVE OF GOD
Or Love of A Higher Power

God is a word of infinite interpretations . . .   In this book — this body of thought — it mainly means a Higher Power . . .   a Force bigger than we are . . .   Can anyone doubt there is such a Force? When we look at the magnificence of our own body, the workings of our own mind, to say nothing of the millions of people on the Planet, a Planet set in a sky amidst millions of other planets, as well as other stars and universes, how can we ever doubt that there is a Higher Power than we are? . . .   Man has yet to make a worm! . . . . He may be getting close to it but he's not there yet, and even if he gets there, he's got an infinitely long way to go to be able to accomplish anything nearly as awesome as those wonders of this Higher Power. It has always been amusing to me to observe how, whenever our scientists make a brilliant discovery, they are then eulogized and rewarded for their discovery . . .   I have no quarrel with honoring the scientists for their works. They should be honored. But when the discovery is made, no one seems to credit the Creator whose work they have discovered . . .   People don't create what they discover. Discovery means finding something that was already there.

Let me share a story with you . . .   Back in the late 1700's a group of French engineers were strolling in Rosetta, Egypt. As they walked along, they passed a flat slab, a large stone half buried in the mud, and one of them said, "Look at that stone . . .   all covered with glacier scratches." They all took a sideways glance, but one of the men, lingering, looked carefully at the marks on the stone. He realized that these markings were not merely glacier scratches but were probably some kind of writing . . .   Later, a French scholar deciphered the 3 languages that were on that stone, one of which was Egyptian hieroglyphics. This in turn opened up a whole new vista of history.

The point of this story is that if the markings on that stone had been only glacier scratches, no one could have deciphered them into a language. It was only because they had been put there by a "Mind" that another "mind" could decipher them. It is my view that the scientists with their minds are uncovering the work that the Mind of a Higher Power has already done. Scientific discoveries always point to the reality of a Higher Power, something greater and beyond what we humans have.

Since it seems to me that it is *self-evident* there is a Higher Power, as evident as dirt or trees, we would surely do well to discuss the *Nature* of this power. Is it with us, or against us? It again seems self-evident that any Power which could create human beings capable of being loving, (even as well as being non-loving), must in and of its own Being, be at least capable of Love, the highest form of Love . . . What is the highest form of Love?

The highest form of Love I have known is the kind of Love that accepts the difficult experience of non-love, but tries to inspire and transform that non-love, be it in a person or an event, into Love. So, if we accept the *logic* of a Higher Power that is loving, but allows non-love to exist, even as that Power calls us in our deepest selves to be loving, then can we not love this Power or Creator because it's essence is loving, and because it is giving us each a life-chance to struggle to learn to be loving ourselves? If we were not given the choice to choose to be non-loving as well as loving, we would never learn the value of love, or the fact we feel better and healthier when we are loving than when we are not . . .

Theologians throughout the ages have wrestled with how we could have a loving Creator when that Creator allows evil or non-love to exist. Doesn't the answer lie in the fact we are intended to be co-Creators, turning non-love to love? If the opposite of

Love did not exist, we would have no free will at all, and we could not be co-Creators of Love. It may seem a bit difficult, but isn't it a high honor to have been placed in a Creation where our challenge is to change non-love to Love and to be co-Creators?

Whether or not we can accept this Higher Power, this Creator or God, and His/Her challenge to us to change non-love to Love, it is very important to decide, because loving and trusting this Supreme Power affects our basic motivation, and it therefore influences how we live and love with our 3 other Loves; Love of Self, Love of Other, and Love of All.

If, as individuals or a Society, we are going to have any cohesive meaning to life, we are going to have to recognize this Higher Power *and* the Nature of it. Otherwise we have a Society of individual egos "full of sound and fury," running around and clashing in their own little worlds of their own little wants and desires, rather than a Society pulling together to make this Planet work. So let's now look at the other 3 Loves, starting with "Love of Self," in order to better understand the fullness and cohesiveness of Love. The 4-Loves seem inextricably intertwined. Understanding these Loves and how they interact will reinforce the importance of our love of this Higher Power.

LOVE OF SELF

We can love our Selves by making the difficult effort to talk to our Selves, saying: "Look at me, I'm great, pretty, handsome, confident, capable," etc., or we can love our Self simply because we are a child of, a magnificent Creation of, this Higher Power. Love of the Higher Power does affect the ease and stability with which we are able to love and value our Selves. When we love this Creator, this Higher Power, we have an *indestructible basic identity* in that we are a child of this Creator just as much as anyone else . . . .and no one can take our identity away from us. Whereas, when we rely for our identity and self-esteem only on our Selves . . . our moods, our ups and downs, they can plummet us.

Here are some more of the ways that loving our Creator affects the way we love our Self:

1.   Loving our Creator or the Higher Power, affects not only our identity and self-esteem but as we said, *our motivation*, because to honor our own gift of life, we know we want to struggle to be the unique person we are. We never want to let our loving Creator down, by not fulfilling the energy and gifts He entrusted us with. No two of us have even fingerprints alike, so each of us can always be motivated by the fact we have not only a loving Creator to serve, but a unique role to play as we do that. However great or simple that role, we are the only one who can live it. That is a pretty special challenge, and one we can each care about. Each of us comes with a vision inside of how we can make things better . . . We need to be true to that vision and make it happen . . .

2. In loving a loving Higher Power we have a way to never feel guilty, and that is by asking our Creator's forgiveness, sincerely intending not to repeat whatever we have done that was unloving. In loving the Higher Power therefore, we can forgive our Selves, because by sincerely *asking* for forgiveness, we have been told by the greatest teacher of Love on Earth that we *are* forgiven.

3. We can love our Selves better if we recognize that we have not only been given a loving side, but a non-loving side as well, and that *our task is to keep in touch with our loving side* even as we stumble and do non-loving things. Love of our Creator anchors us, and thereby frees us to keep working toward being our most real, most loving and highest Selves. An anchored ship can ride out a storm, whereas an unanchored ship is likely to crash on the shore.

4. Loving our Creator also makes it possible for the Self to say in those hardest of moments, those terrible moments when we *must humbly give up* and let go of something we care deeply about, "Not my will but Thine be done." We can do this more easily knowing that we love our Creator and our Creator loves us, than we can in the alternate situation of having no feelings of a larger Being with Whom to share our life struggle.

Additionally, when we have had to give up something or someone we care about, we have the resource of being able to *trust* this Higher Power to open new doors for us, doors through which we can go in Love. Learning to trust this Higher Power's Love of each of us, and knowing a new door of Love will open, takes openness and waiting. In loving a Higher Power we can walk with deeper strength as we go about both loving and fulfilling our own unique Self.

5. So many of us who don't believe in a loving Higher Power, and who therefore have no sense of identity, are angry—furious—and without even recognizing it, we look at life as not being good to us, not being fair to us. We therefore are vulnerable and lock into non-loving "Causes" just for the sake of identity: street gangs, drug gangs, Neo-Nazis, the Ku-Klux Klan . . . and many others that are less blatant and violent, serve this identity need. But they are all equally non-loving for us as individuals, and for Society . . .

6. "Be still and know that I am God" . . . we must not let our non-loving feelings scare us . . . When we look inside, remember we all, *deepest* down, want "to love, be loved and be productive."
We are all truly beautiful at the innermost core of our Selves, so our non-loving feelings must exist for a purpose. We are challenged to turn these feelings to love . . . So often we don't want to look within and discover our God, our Higher Power, and our deepest wish . . . which is our Common Goal. We deny both it and our negative and non-loving feelings, projecting them onto others, blaming them, or blaming society . . . Let's let it be fun to be in touch with our deepest Self, our Higher Power . . . They are the same. Then Love of God and what He has obviously set in motion for us as task, causes us to be eager to be creative, instead of afraid.

7. You have heard a glass can be said to be half-empty or half-full . . . In my view, conviction about a loving God is what makes the difference. Isn't it possible that loving God flips our attitude from negative to positive, thereby making us feel healthier and more creative . . . and that in turn affects our whole Society?
Some people call conviction about this obvious Higher Power a weakness. They say

people need it for a prop. In answer to those critics, I'd like to say that in life there are many tough choices we have to make when it is *harder* to be loving, to take the loving path, than it is to take a non-loving, inconsiderate, self-focused, self-indulgent path . . .

Loving a loving Creator is a matter of logic, conviction — not a "leap of faith" — and it makes loving one's Self far more logical and stable than egocentric love. Also important, it provides us with a sounder base from which to love an Other.

LOVE OF OTHER

This is definitely the most difficult and complex Love that is required of us in our effort to be loving. The reason is there are so many variables in the people we try to love that we have real difficulty in understanding them. Unless those people communicate well and tell us what is going on inside them, what they are thinking and feeling, what their motives are, it is impossible for us to know. *We cannot accurately second-guess an Other*. Here are some of the variables that we need to try to discover and be aware of:

First, we must try to discover where someone is in his or her own personal Journey, in either their insights, their ideas, or their competencies, and therefore, what we can hope to count on from them. We all think that because *we* understand something that the other does too, but it has been learned the hard way that "The Other cannot know what he does not know." This fact makes imputing motives to another, which we are all prone to do, taboo . . .

We must always *ask* the Other what he thinks and needs . . .   We must always *ask* what an Other is feeling and what his motivation is. We must respect the Other as an Other child of our Creator, wherever in their Journey they happen to be, and harder yet, sometimes we can only wait for them to discover for themselves where they are, and for *them* to want to share what's going on, with *us*. As the Faith At Work group so aptly phrased it, "The door has to open from inside." We cannot force communication upon an Other. Great communication is a matter of *mutual* desire.

Instead of the world being full of perfect people, we have a world full of growing people, all at different stages, and all with different or confused world views. We also have a world of people with different gifts and different languages. It is truly hard to understand other people, and hard to try to deal with them.

Having been a sea-shell collector for many years, when I first began collecting shells, I was always looking for the most perfect shell, and that pleasurable excitement occupied me for many, many years. I always ignored the broken ones, as did everyone else. The whole milieu of the shell world was to find the perfect shell. And then one day a friend of mine took me in to see a man who had just lost his wife, and to my surprise, his wife had collected nothing but broken shells. As my friend unfolded his story about her, she had three children, each of whom was handicapped. One was born a congenital cripple, one was schizophrenic, and one was an alcoholic. This woman did not look for perfect shells. She picked up broken shells, and then, with these, she made little statues or dancing figures, using also broken twigs and pieces of coral. Her sculpturing work was a delight. To have known this Mother's work was a real life revelation for me, because it made me aware of the fact that we human beings are all, to a degree, broken shells. And when we try to understand and love one an Other, we need to remember this story and be challenged as was that Mother, to turn imperfect pieces to delightful results . . . to help everyone feel more loved and be more productive.

This broken shells story has also helped me solve an issue in loving Others, that I personally have found very difficult, and that is the issue of loyalty. So many people hope you will be loyal to them no matter what . . . This is true even among nations. In the Persian Gulf War when King Hussein of Jordan took a position on behalf of the Iraqis and Sadaam Hussein, it upset a lot of our leaders because they felt he was being disloyal to the Coalition . . . This story about broken shells has helped me to see that because we are all incomplete in our wholeness and lovingness, that although we can be a true friend to someone, we cannot be blindly and *totally* loyal about what they do or think . . . We have to be honest enough to recognize where they are, and try to assess whether we think they are loving or not. And we need to be able to take a position that tells them exactly that. If we say "I am your friend and I think you are wonderful at this, this, and this, but what you're doing here in this part of your life feels un-loving or negative to me and it upsets me," at least then we evoke a dialogue that helps bring *real* understanding, and helps us solve this dilemma of how and where we can be loyal.

"Oh wad some power the giftie gie us
To see oursels as others see us."
—Robert Burns

My grandson has a sign on his bedroom door that says: "Be gentle with me. God is not finished with me yet."

People are very fragile and easily hurt, and we must never forget that. And some people who are hurt, become bullies, bravados, in order to cover up their hurt. So we have another dilemma; how can we handle bullies? Surely we must stand strong with bullies and not let them push us around unfairly. But even as we do stand strong against them, we must be trying to evoke their loving side. We need to work exhaustively to reach the best in another person, even as we stand strongly against whatever he or she is doing that we feel is non-loving. When we persist in this, we usually win for both of us. Never forget, what we all want is "to love, be loved and be productive."

Lastly, the most important insight in dealing with incomplete Others is knowing how to forgive them . . . It has helped me, to understand that forgiveness is a *feeling* of Love that operates on 2 levels . . . On one level, we can forgive in our own heart, no matter what the Other does, knowing he is growing, and *that* keeps *us* free of pain and bitterness . . . But on the 2nd level—the level of relating—only if the Other communicates with us, and asks for our forgiveness, can the *relationship* be healed. So one part of forgiveness is for our own well-being. The other is what causes the relationship to be healed, and is a matter of communication.

Loving an Other, any Other, requires the trust that God is about Love, plus Love of Self, plus ongoing communication with that Other. But is there a greater joy than satisfactorily relating to an Other?

> *"All who joy would win*
> *Must share it—happiness was born a twin."*
> —Lord Byron

LOVE OF ALL

Love of All is basically an *attitude* of Love towards All, because of course we cannot possibly know All . . .   However, in trying to think about what is most loving for a family, or group, or community, or nation, we do raise a question that often puts the desires, rights and freedoms of the Self in tension with what is best for All. I have always called this the "Pro-Self, Pro-Social" tension . . .   So often our hardest times are when we have to deny our Selves, for the good of All . . .

Perhaps in a troublesome situation, by just asking, "What is loving of God, Self, Other and All it will give us a kind of divine sense of humor, because the asking of it detaches us from getting too intense and we can see and laugh at our own foibles as well as those of Others.

Some of the kinds of questions, that in loving All, are apt to set up "Pro-Self, Pro-Social" tensions are:

1. Should television have the unrebuked freedom to show violence and nudity and low tastes and standards in dress and language, and bring these into our living rooms when it is known such imaging does affect our children and unstable adults adversely? Freedom to express, to be Pro-Self, often opposes the well being of All—the Community. Of course if the expressing Self is co-creating with all 4-Loves in mind or heart, then that Self's expression usually does not offend the ''All''—the Community.

2 . Should we really make *laws* by majority vote instead of by unanimous vote?

3. Should women who choose to have children and who *want* to work full time, give up having children for the good of the children?

Despite our awareness and increased understanding of 4-Loves loving we must never get away from, or let go of the *feeling* of love . . .   Some say they don't know what love is and ask, "What is the feeling of Love like?" To find out it is best to get back in touch with some inspiring experience we have had, or think about someone we have truly loved. Think of our love for a puppy perhaps, or the smell of a gardenia, or gardening, or a deeply moving piece of music, or a sunset, a child, or some adult person we have loved and admired . . .

Get hold of that *feeling* of love and hang onto it. Think of it as not only the deepest feeling within us but also as a strong Thread we can reach out for and grab. Think of it as a line stretching from our deepest selves to the Highest Power in the universe, and back again. For in the act of *thinking* about our Common Goal and 4-Loves balancing, we are apt to lose that all important *feeling* of love, which feeling infuses and changes and colors our whole approach to Loving. In fact, its presence or absence clues us as to whether we are on the Love track, or off. We sometimes reduce it to the idea of conscience, but it is more than that. It is a warm, infusing feeling of Love.

When I watch so many of the preachers or teachers of Love on television, or in pulpits, I am often struck by the fact that these people don't come through to me as *being* loving, or *feeling* love. They often shout, which turns me off. Love is gentle. Love is infectious. It is joyous, uplifting, a kind of feeling that is not condemning or threatening . . .

Also, Love is not sex . . .   Ideally, the highest form of sex, the most fulfilling form of sex, follows 4-Loves loving and respect for an Other . . .   It is not an "I/It" relationship, but an "I/Thou" relationship . . .   Think what a far cry such caring and feeling is from rape . . .   Sex has nothing to do with the 4-Loves loving we are reaching for here . . . Sex is a separate *addition* to Love, which *ideally* follows the 4-Loves loving.

If ever we are feeling non-love in relation to an Other, or All, I have found a process I call "Balloon Brainstorming" which helps me to pin-point the source of my non-love. I go off alone, take a large art pad and write across the top: "What's bugging me?" Meaning: why am I not feeling loving about this? (whatever or whoever it is). I then let my resultant thoughts flow across my mind . . .   I jot each one down on the pad in a helter-skelter, not-linear fashion. I then put a circle around each isolated thought or notion . . .   The pad begins to look like a question with a lot of balloons floating around below it . . .   Then because I have gotten all my thoughts and feelings out on that pad, I can look at them objectively and, in seeing them, they are clearer to me than when they were bottled up in my head . . .   I can then sift and synthesize them until I clearly and visually *see* what is bugging me . . .   After that, I can develop a positive loving alternate to them, which I can then substitute in my thinking for the muddle I was experiencing . . .   Result? Immediate relief . . .   I can now go on with understanding and with an inner calm, and be genuinely fully loving . . .

So with an understanding of Love as 4-Loves, and with a way to get in touch with and hang onto our love *feeling,* our Common Goal of wanting to "love, be loved, and be productive" becomes the unifying and inspiring guideline we have been looking for . . . None of us has all the answers, and the answers will keep changing. We can only keep struggling to search honestly for the loving answers.

But we can now view our Common Goal as what deep down we all want, what is healthy, the Missing Piece in the Jig-saw Puzzle of Life, and even as the given fundamental Reality that unites the world . . . To pay attention to it is the only satisfying way to find cohesive direction, to figure out and put joyfully together the Players, and the Parts and Pieces of Life.

CHAPTER 3

Our Common Goal
And The "Eyes To See"

    Having progressed a little towards understanding better what loving with our Common Goal balanced by 4-Loves means, I want to share with you how trying to actually live out of this perspective, has given me the "Eyes to See." It has given me the "Eyes to See" and find the ways that can correct our personal and social ills. I have discovered that this perspective gives any of us who are aware of it a way to discern priorities, see cause and effect, see what is on the love track and what is off . . . see what in our relations is undesirably unilateral and what is mutual.

Long ago this new way of seeing revealed to me the truth and importance of Erik Erikson's *8 Stages of Growth,* the eight milestones through which we all pass. I believe Erik Erikson delineated something more potent than perhaps he realized when he described these 8 Stages, not only because they are so obviously true, but also because he was pointing out the importance of *how* we pass through them. If we go through them feeling loved, we are given the gift of emotional health and well being; and if we are not so blessed, we have to make up for that later.

The 8 stages Erikson described are: the **Stage of Infancy**, or being newborn. It is here that we receive either a basic sense of trust or mistrust of life. If we feel cared for and our infant needs—such as thirst, hunger, dry diapers, cuddling, eye contact, and play—are met, as against the fear of being abandoned or neglected, we go through this stage with a solid emotional base, ready for the next stage of life which is called The Toddler Stage.

In the **Toddler Stage**, we begin to develop a will of our own, a sort of autonomy, or a beginning of autonomy, as opposed to what many children experience at this time—shame and doubt. When a child of that age jumps up on something like a little low wall or step, so proud of himself that he can do it, instead of his parents saying "Hey, Johnny, that's great—look what you can do!" We are apt to hear them say "No, no, no! Get down, you'll hurt yourself." Or worse, they may say to him: "You should be ashamed of yourself. You know you ought not to do that." So just as the little bud of autonomy, or a will of his own, is beginning to grow, it gets emotionally nipped, so that the Toddler loses good feelings about his growth and independence, which is what he and his parents should be about at this time.

The next milestone is the **Young Child Stage** where Erikson points out that the child begins to develop either initiative or mistrust of his abilities, or worse, guilt about himself. When he doesn't have support for his initiatives in this stage, when he's has been scolded too much and negated too much, the discouraged child has been heard to say, "I'm just a bad creepy child and I hate myself." I actually heard a four-year-old say those words one day, and was immediately reminded of Erikson. I couldn't believe it.

Next is the stage of **The Older Child**, who begins to develop even more complex competencies, as opposed to a feeling of inferiority. The fact is, Erikson says, this issue of trust versus mistrust, confidence vs. no confidence comes up at every stage along the way.

And then there is the **Youth Stage**, in which the beginnings of real identity begin. A young person begins to feel he is "good at this," or "not good at that," and he begins to sense his own unique Self in contrast to the confusion of not knowing who he really is. At this stage, if he has the proper confidence and emotional security given him by loving parents and surrounding teachers, he will have the courage to take chances and learn more about himself.

Next comes the **Stage of Young Adulthood**. This is a very important stage, because at this point we learn to share ourselves in *intimacy* —in *mutuality*—with another person. If something happens in that period to prevent our developing secure and loving feelings, we don't properly learn how to be intimate and mutual with an Other. It doesn't mean we can not get on top of it later, it just means we have to work at replacing all those negative feelings that have been given us. So many of our marriages are in trouble today, particularly because in this crucial stage of growth our men have been raised primarily to have pride, to be brave, to go onward and upward, and they have not learned the comfortableness of being able simply to cry, to be human, to share their hurts, and get their pain out. These men (it can be women too) bottle up their feelings, "numb out," as John Bradshaw says, and develop blind spots. They then lose touch with what they really feel. As adults, we are apt to "act-out" these buried feelings, not really understanding why. St. Paul's "I do what I would not, and do not do what I would" probably fits here. This often includes feelings of loneliness, and isolation, even from someone we love.

Erikson then goes on to point out that in the **Middle-Adult** years if all is going well, we are creative and productive in our jobs or professions, and also good mates and parents in our homes.

And finally, in **Old Age** he points out that all that we have experienced and endured in life, sort of comes together in an integration of understanding. He said we then develop "a creative symphony of life, as versus despair," and that this helps us "to accept even death . . . "

Interestingly, it was the *feeling* of love in me that I know caused me to prick up my senses and recognize the great thing that this man Erikson had done. He had contributed an enormous understanding to how and why we grow as we do, and made clear the intrinsic importance of *prevailing* love to health and happiness at every step of the way. This in turn made clear to me the importance of how we raise our children.

Trying to live out of the *feeling* of love, balanced by the 4-Loves has caused me to also be aware of more of the brilliant insights of John Bradshaw, who is at the time of this writing, sharing with the public on television his programs and workshops (*Homecoming*, produced for PBS by KQED). It is interesting to note that he uses Erikson's 8 stages as a base for getting in touch with what he calls our "wounded inner-child." He points out that all the emotional difficulties people carry within themselves, or experience with one another in adult life, usually stem from hurts acquired in one of these 8 stages . . . And he points out the essential activity that each of us must go through in order to get in touch with these "wounds," and do what he calls "Original Pain Work." In other words, he says that now that we are grown, we can help our little inner-child who was damaged growing up to understand what happened to him, and to replace the unloving things that happened with new under-standing of the Love that he should have gotten, or wished for.

In recognizing what our inner child was denied, and "grieving over it," literally crying and crying until we cry out the hurt, we experience an "immediate healing." Bradshaw says this grieving is the only way to free up our blind and "numb" spots. Once we have re-experienced our Original Pain, and gotten it out, shared it with a trusted friend or counselor, only then can we instill the new and desired Love feelings in our psyche.

What Bradshaw has come to see and verbalize is powerful and brilliant, and we're very lucky to have him out there helping us to learn how to overcome our emotional repressions, our compulsions, our guilts, our "numbed out" blockages, our ignorance of our Selves, so we can be free to be *spontaneous* and *mutually* loving, without need for domination or manipulation, without need to wear a mask or conform instead of being real and living out of substance. How many of us conform, or *per*form, rather than take the time to know what we really feel, so that we do live out of substance instead of compliancy or falseness?

A third concept 4-Loves loving has caused me to become aware of, "to see," is a problem-solving technique called the Conflict Resolution Process. I see this Process as the Center Jewel of all human relating. Let me tell you why I feel this way about it. First of all, it is a very simple process, but it truly works for people—all people. It works for people who do not trust each other, as well as for people who do, and this is what makes it so very important. It works because if you use it correctly, it forces two people to learn what it means to relate. *We all think we relate.* But this Process causes us to *really* relate.

What it amounts to is three simple basic steps:

1. When two people come together, we will call one the Initiator, the other the Responder. The Initiator says something, and whatever he/she says, the other person responds to him/her. If the Responder feels provoked, or defensive, angry, or ready to retaliate, it is at this point that the Responder must "hold his horses" and move on to the second step.

2. Instead of defending himself, the Responder must first make the Initiator *feel heard.* It is natural to want to defend or argue when someone has said something provocative to us, but if the Responder, instead of reacting defensively, makes the Initiator *feel heard,* that is, gets the Initiator saying: "Yes, that is what I mean," then the Initiator's bristles go down . . . And once the Initiator believes the Responder is understanding him, he will say in several ways, "yes, that is what I mean."
    This Process of 1) *listening,* and 2) making the Other *feel heard* is essential, and constitutes the first two steps of the Process. To complete the second step, the Process

must then be reversed, and the Responder has his turn to say what he feels about the issue that has just been raised. The original Initiator, instead of arguing back, reciprocates with the same courtesy—he makes the Responder *feel heard.*

So now you have two people who have stated opposing points of view, or at least differing points of view, and who have really caused each other to feel heard and understood . . . These first two steps should be done over and over until both feel clear about what their issue really is. When two people thus *feel heard and understood* by each other, and feel they see their issue clearly, they are ready to take the third step which is to begin to find solutions to the problem.

3. The best way I know to do this is to have a large art pad, sheet of paper, blackboard, whatever you can find handy, and each one of you start to think about a solution that would work for *both* of you, not just one of you, *both* of you. And now, knowing how the Other feels, when you find a solution that you feel might work for both of you, you put this on the pad. Each person should try to come up with at least two or three solutions that they earnestly believe might work for *both* of them.

The reason this begins to work magic in solving differences and conflicts, is because the two people who understand each other *for the first time*, really try to think about what not only solves their *own* problem but what might solve the other person's problem too. These two people "own" their joint problem, and they are the only ones who can find solutions that work for both of them. If nothing is accomplished with the first set of suggested solutions, new sets of suggestions should be written on the pad until a satisfactory solution is found.

A wonderful story along this line is that there were two men who wanted to buy the same orange orchard and they got into a big hassle about it, each one arguing about who got there first and why he should have it. To complicate matters further they each had lawyers involved. When the Conflict Resolution Process was introduced to them and they used it, they discovered in the third step, in trying to think about what would work for *both* of them, that one of them wanted the products that came from the juice of the oranges, and the other wanted a chemical that came from the rind of the oranges. In this case they were able to buy the orchard together.

I don't know if that is a true story or not, but it is one that is told in Conflict Resolution circles. It may not be totally accurate the way I've told it but it is a good example of the kind of thing that causes rejoicing, because a *new* solution is found out of caring for *both*, which never would have occurred had they remained in a locked-horns position.

This Process is truly magic, and it is worth noting that it initially comes out of respect for the Other, and then caring for the Other . . . both of which are derivatives of recognizing our Common Goal. It is also worth noting that if ever you find yourself in a defensive argument, know one of you failed to make the Initiator *feel heard*. Take responsibility for that and use the Process.

There is always the possibility that if the two people cannot hear each other and clarify their issue, they can at this point find a mediator to help them. Mediation is a very helpful and constructive way to go.

Another of the factors that make this Process seem like magic and cause it to work is the fact that the two people learn to be totally *mutual*. There is no dominating figure in this Process . . . . Sometimes, even though there is no domination existing in the Process, there can actually exist between the two people the fact that one has more money, or one has more power, or some other imbalance, but if they truly give themselves to the Process, knowing that neither will lose and both will win, they discover the real joy there is in solving conflict with a verbal process, instead of with power, verbal abuse, or worse, with violence.

Using this Process keeps us on the Track of being Loving, by forcing us to understand our issues, instead of just being defensive and argumentative. Because of this new positioning in relation to one an-Other, solutions are truly new creations, created in the moment of caring for the Other as well as one's Self.

Some people say the Process is unnatural, and that they "would rather fight," or that they "want to win." But that doesn't last long if we think of our loving Creator . . . Either the Logic of there being a loving Creator, or the Self-interest in recognizing losers retaliate, will cause us to try to cooperate, to try to use the Process.

Is the Process unnatural? To answer this, consider learning to drive an automobile. None of us are born knowing how to operate an automobile. When we first learn, we have to think about where the gears are, where the brake is, where the lights are, whatever, and we have to do that until we know it by heart, at which point it becomes automatic for us. It becomes so automatic that after a short time when we drive, we think about anything we want. We think about where we are going to dinner, what we want to do in a business deal, and so forth . . .

Just so! We are not born knowing how to use the Conflict Resolution Process, but once we learn it, it becomes automatic for us and we find ourselves, even when the other person isn't consciously using it with us, we find ourselves trying to understand the Other, and reach solutions that consider the Other. Even such a one-sided effort usually helps enormously. Of course if the issue is real and vital, both people should know the Process, and have someone be sure they use it properly, and use it consciously. When someone says something provocative to us, instead of responding defensively, we say:

"Oh, is that what you are thinking? Let's talk about it."

If you need to make a confronting remark to an-Other, say:

"I hope you will listen to what I want to say to you, *will you*?" Then follow the Conflict Resolution Process, together.

Never forget what a good healthy relationship is like. A good healthy give-and-take relationship is *mutual,* non-dominating, win-win. It is an easy, nimble, humble, light back and forth verbal exchange, and a true joy . . .

Another impediment to using the Process is that people often don't want to learn something new. Most of us resist change. But if the change is toward being more loving and having more fun winning for both, instead of one losing (remember, losers usually retaliate), why not be *eager* to change? Of course the reason could be we have a childhood or youth blockage we need to discover, and deal with . . . or we are experiencing a moment of greed, hurt or anger. Otherwise it is reasonable, isn't it, to want the joy of being loved and getting along with people? It will be a new day for all of us when this Process is taught in our schools.

Loving and being in touch with the *feeling* of love leads not only to joy but to actual competence in whatever we do. There is something fundamental in the human psyche that when it is feeling heard and understood, it is creative and joyful, whereas if it is feeling blocked, frustrated, or misunderstood, it becomes miserable and just doesn't perform well.

There is another whole area, which in trying to love with 4-Loves, keeping in touch with the love feeling, that during my lifetime I have come to think deeply about. For even if we are able to overcome our own emotional shortcomings and blockages from childhood, and we've learned how to use the Conflict Resolution Process, we still have to deal with the kind of Communities we live in and their Systems that influence us. Communities and their Systems either reinforce the loving side of people or work towards its detriment. I think it was Winston Churchill who once said, "We build our institutions, and then our institutions build us." The same thing is true with our Communities and our cities. We build our Communities and cities, and then they build us.

When I was young, in my early married years with young children, I had everything supposedly that a young woman could ask for; a lovely suburban place, a successful husband, wonderful children, but I felt something was missing, that there was something sterile about my day-to-day existence. It eventually boiled down to the fact that I was very lonely. In those days there was no way to get around the suburbs except by automobile, and many of us from my generation discovered we were endlessly driving children to schools, to dentists, to doctors, to art classes, to friends' houses . . . and our own need to be in relationship with other people our own age was stifled. The result was that many of us were very lonely. A solution that some of us discovered was that in the summers when we went to swimming pools and the children were all happy in the pool, the adults did have time to talk with each other, and this made a tremendous difference in our own enjoyment of life. We all need someone with whom we can share daily life and living.

This set me to thinking about how we could design Communities in such a way that young mothers who worked at home and were doing good jobs with their kids could have more adult companionship, and I began to realize that an ideal way to live was to have seven to nine families living in a cul-de-sac where the young children could play together, perhaps on the front side of the house, and on the back side the young family could have privacy, as the yard stretched out into more and more country . . . .

This thinking of small Community living became a focus of mine and I began to also apply it in the realm of shopping. I hated having to go to one big store in one section of the city for one thing, then going somewhere else for another and I began to yearn to have a small village-type Community in which there were many small-scaled shops. The result of this yearning and thinking led to the building of such a community as Cross Keys in Baltimore, Maryland and that in turn became a kind of microcosm for a neighborhood in the now well-known town of Columbia, Maryland.

Along with this need for the small scale cul-de-sac and Community, where children could walk or bicycle to school, and where parents had more companionship, came the realization that there were two periods in the life of a growing family, in which a full City Center was needed. One was when teenagers grew beyond their small-scale Neighborhoods and Villages and were seeking a meeting spot or something a little farther afield. The other was when parents reached the post-parental period and needed city stimulation and excitement.

Having lived in New York City during my twentieth year, I thought about how wonderful it would be if we could build small-scale Neighborhoods and Villages around a city center. This would give the advantages of everything to the family growth cycle. So this became the basic schema for Columbia, Maryland. (see Appendix)

After beginning to see that the basic *Design* of cities would help the growth of families, I began to realize that all the *Systems* within the city also affected the emotional health and well being of those who lived there. The Systems that needed to be looked at out of 4-Loves loving, are well known to all of us. One is our Governments, the way we elect officials and have them represent us. Shouldn't our Communities be small enough that we actually know our elected local officials in their daily lives? . . . It does seem impersonal to select people we don't even know . . . Television now helps us to know those who represent larger areas—state and national—and television can do even more with this need to better know our governmental representatives. Interviews by savvy people are far more informative than debates. Debates focus more on besting the opponent than on offering solutions to issues.

We also know our School Systems are far too large and that they are not evoking the best in our children. I believe each school needs to think about what is *loving* and *fun* at each of the Erikson stages of growth and base its Systems of Development and Teaching on that. "When you love someone, you evoke their gifts," said Gordon Cosby of the Church of the Saviour in Washington, D.C. At this time, our school systems are extremely overcrowded and as a result, force our children through programs whether or not they fit with the students' gifts or needs.

Our Economic System certainly has many flaws and very often does not work to elicit creativity in people and make it possible for their talents to flower. Need or greed for money so often becomes a blockage to the best in us, constricts us instead of freeing us. Making money so often becomes a competitor to Loving. So surely our Economic System ought to be looked at, as to whether it is loving for people or not. "Economics should be made for man, not man for economics" . . . One of the biggest problems we all face of course is the population explosion. We have far too many people on Earth already, and we don't know yet how many people are ideal for defined regional areas. All of these things about Cities and Systems need to be considered in the light of the *feeling* of love balanced by 4-Love loving.

It would be beneficial if all our Cities could be broken into small communities of 2-300, the city part being a City Center. Then we could have both a City Forum and

Community Forums which would be made up of volunteer citizens, who would keep abreast of ongoing concerns in that City or Community, and who would keep constant check on whether or not the Systems of that City or Community were helping every person "to love, be loved, and be productive."

It would also be great if every City had a "Center For Human Understanding," which was a sort of World's Fair "Pavilion of Life," where it's youth and citizens could go to learn or be refreshed about our Common Goal, 4-Loves loving, and the Conflict Resolution Process. This Pavilion would be essentially a *preventive* resource, a joyous way to learn how to love and relate and deal with all our relationships . . . It could be a place that would remind us of the meaning in our lives and uplift us . . . It could also offer practical courses in such subjects as: How to Pick a Mate; the Nature of Marriage; How to Parent—subjects that are missing in today's learning curricula.

When we think of the common problems of drug addiction, violence, teenage pregnancy, loneliness and homelessness, crime and meaninglessness, it is clear that the Design and Systems of our Communities must be changed. Where we live must be small, human-scale, with access to City Centers, where both the Design and Systems reinforce our capacity to love, rather than deteriorate it.

I can be wrong, but I have a strong personal conviction that when a family raises a child or children, that family should own a small piece of land—at least 1/4 acre. This indicts all of our cities for child raising . . . but I am convinced that a child raised in touch with Nature, so they can garden and have the responsibility of pets, is a child grounded and rooted in values of awe and wonder. It gives them a deep root in the spiritual value of care and nurturing another live creature, and being responsible for the consequences of that creature's well being . . . It also keeps a child busy in a wholesome way . . . Children who grow up in concrete and brick with a few trees planted here and there, who think no further than that milk comes from a carton, have lost both hours well spent and an essential training in values, self-confidence, and beginning relationships. It seems to me that instead of adults pushing their city life-styles on children, we should be guided in our design and development by the *children's needs* and joys. Adults can move to Cities' Centers if they want to, after their children grow up.

A few *scattered* observations I have discovered in trying to live out of our Common Goal and 4-Loves loving are:

1. There really should be no use of the words good/bad, right/wrong, in reference to the Inner Self or to Human Relations, but only the words, loving and non-loving. To observe this use of words, gets us out of a lot of controversial moments. We can argue forever about whether someone or something is right/wrong, good/bad, but there is a whole new note of concern when we wrestle with whether something is loving or non-loving . . . it becomes more personal, more mutual, and more human.

2. Another observation worth noting is that inherent in our very existence, inherent in the fact that when we do relate to one another, there are two ways in which we must inevitably hurt one another.
—one is when we choose a mate.
—another is when we choose our friends . . .

In these two situations, we are bound to hurt Others.

Fortunately, when we do get hurt there are many people around, "other fish in the sea," so we learn to move on and find a different mate, or other friends. However, these can be moments of given intrinsic pain . . . It is very important to be aware of this *human pitfall*, and not to enlarge it with attributions of racism or privilege, etc . . . These hurts happen to all of us . . .

> *He drew a circle that shut me out*
> *Heretic, rebel, a thing to flout.*
> *But love and I had the wit to win.*
> *We drew a circle that took him in.*
> —Edwin Markham

And lastly, recognition of our Common Goal gives us the "Eyes to See" *what questions to ask and pursue.* So often I find people or groups spinning their wheels, because they have no reference point . . . It is as though they get mired in the mud and ask questions therefore about the mud, rather than how to get out of the mud to a better place. But if we ask our questions in reference to our Common Goal, The 4-Loves, and with the *feeling* of love, then we stay on a productive and rewarding track . . . I believe that such historic episodes as the Crusades, Witch-hunts, and Jim Jones scenarios would never have taken place had such guidelines been operative.

Seeing with the "Eyes of Love" is the only way to have "Eyes that See."

CHAPTER 4

A CLEAR CALL ...

If we are going to correct our relational and social ills, eradicating drug abuse, child abuse, violence, teen pregnancy, murders, loneliness, homelessness, joblessness, meaningless communities and systems, environmental pollution, and have more joy in our lives, we need to work on all of the following frontiers all at once and all the time ... We each, and I emphasize *each*, need to:

1. *Recognize and verbalize our Common Goal*. Share it and mean it as our motive, or deny it. Behavior comes most often out of motive and we need to be clear about our motive, first with our Self and then with one an Other. We need to center on our Common Goal and express it in order to have integrity and to inform . . . telling the whole truth, and nothing but the truth . . .

2. *Keep in touch with our love **feeling***. We must not only balance all we think, say, and do with the 4-Loves, but also with the 4-Loves feeling

3. *Work toward a world that is child-centered*. In order to maintain the feeling of love, we must view every child as a sacred trust. We don't want to allow our Parents, or our Communities and their Systems, to develop Hitlers or Sadaam Husseins . . . We must recognize there are no "enemies" just "wounded children" in adult clothing. We must give all prospective parents courses in parenting. We must learn to listen to our children and their needs for warmth and support . . . their love of pets and Nature—the out of doors.

4. *Be open to learn our own blind or "numb" spots*. Be eager to rid ourselves of these blockages to loving. We must do so by using the Balloon-Brainstorming Process and by turning non-love to Love in our Selves, as well as in outer situations.

5. *Use the Conflict Resolution Process*. Recognize the importance, effectiveness, and magic of the *Conflict Resolution Process* which brings us joyful, *mutual partnerships* without domination, and bring us understanding between husband/wife, parent/child, neighbor/neighbor, boss/employee, nation/nation.

6. *Build and re-build our Communities*. Recognize it will take not only our own efforts, but our Governments' efforts and financial investment in us, *to build and rebuild our Communities and their Systems,* so that they are of small enough scale—not more than 2-300 people—and connected to City Centers. This we must do in order to re-enforce our Common Goal, raise our children healthfully and lovingly, and open new doors to the love, fun, joy, pace and productivity we all want. Each of us must start where we are to build and rebuild *our* Communities' Design *and* Systems all at once.

7. *Evolve a Planetary Spirit*. Above all and in all matters, we humans need to feel a loving Planetary Spirit—one that emerges from our Common Goal, our New One-Mindedness, and we need to begin to live it, and dance it, starting first with our Self and then with any two of us, to Community after Community of us. Such vision, born of Love and applied in Love to whatever we face on this Planet, will synthesize and integrate Life for us, and keep us going from now through the 21st Century . . . if not forever . . . .

We do have a Clear Call.

EPILOGUE

In recognizing all people want to love, be loved, and be productive, and in urging we all get in touch with the feeling of love and live out of that feeling balanced by 4-Loves, I have left out how we humans can survive the natural and immediate frustrations, hurts, and hostilities we experience as we weave our way through this complex, daily fragmentation called "Life."

Jesus, hanging on the cross said, "Father, forgive them for they know not what they do . . . " If *we* can say that, and recognize that *people really do not know what they are doing,* that they are more often ignorant and deprived, rather than non-loving, it will swing us back in touch with the love *feeling*, and make dealing with anger, hurt, and frustration easier. We need to recognize that children *and adults* are *ignorant* of our Common Goal perspective . . . they are not intentionally mean . . . and they need guidance, not fury. St. Paul's, "Be ye angry and sin (non-love) not" suggests the freedom to be angry, and expressive, but not to be unloving to an Other, attitudinally, verbally or violently . . .

A run around the block, punching a pillow, jumping up and down, or a good cry can usually suffice for us until we find the time to use the Balloon Brainstorming Process and can calm down. The idea of hating the sin (non-love) and not the sinner (non-lover) also helps us to be able to express our anger, and to focus on the deed done rather than the perpetrator.

If we allow our Selves to *feel* the love that is deep down in each of us, even when we are angry or hurt, we find we really do not *want* to hurt an Other . . .   We need to right any non-loving episode first with forgiveness in our hearts, then with non-violent, verbal expression of our anger or hurt, and then by using the Conflict Resolution Process . . .   After all, it's just practical sense; we are all better off if we don't let "the sun go down on our wrath." Let's take the time it takes each day to turn our non-love feelings to love feelings. This keeps them from piling up.

Having said all that, we each need, however, to be prepared for the fact that the non-love or hurt side of even the best of people will pop out in the most unexpected moments, for we humans are truly unaware of our wounded inner child and youth-hood patterns . . . and we are also up against the wounds that happen daily in adult life. . . The only way we can keep our Selves from unduly suffering over an Other's ignorant immaturities or their adult pressures and foibles is to recognize these behaviors for what they are.

We must be sure we are open and eager to talk matters over with the Other, and if the Other refuses, that is a sad moment . . .   All we can do is "shake the dust off our feet" and move on . . . We have to leave that relationship to God, and hope that at some future time it can be healed . . . *We* cannot control Others.

Were we all well-trained in our Common Goal perspective as well as the Conflict Resolution Process, we would *prevent* most broken relationships, because we would all know how to talk our issues through to win/win solutions . . .

APPLYING THIS VIEW

Questions And Answers

. . . from friends, acquaintances and just from the inside of my own mind, talking back and forth to itself.

These questions are not organized but at random . . . . The hope is that in giving even these minimal answers (for indeed one could write a volume on most of the questions) the reader will get a sense of how being motivated by our Common Goal guides and directs us to answers and solutions we might otherwise not think of . . . Living out of the perspective of our Common Goal is a habit of the heart, one that heals our hurts, lifts our spirits, teaches us how to relate to Others, build our Families, Family and Friends' Clans, designs our Cities, and guides all of our Systems . . . It changes the way we think and talk, the way we pursue our lives locally and globally.

Philosophical

Q. Somehow, though these ideas sound noble, it bothers me to think of such a lovey-dovey world . . . It sound so boring . . . Part of what makes life interesting is a variety of people and all kinds of problems . . . Eliminate the problems and you have a sort of mush . . . at least that is what I feel . . . Can you help me out of this pudding?

A. Yours is a very natural, human reaction to a deliberate focus more on the love side of life than on the non-love side of life. But don't worry, the non-love realisms of life will keep all of us peppered up . . . This thinking is a call for direction, but it won't eliminate the struggles of daily living . . . Hopefully it will give them a better flavor, but we still have to earn a living, bear and raise children, cope with relationships, cope with illness, accidents, fire and flood, plus it will be a long time before we can actually rebuild our Communities and Systems. There will be long hours of daily work and sadnesses, especially with the population explosion lowering the Quality of Life as it is now doing. However, let me say, that after an unhappy youth period of my own, I enjoyed most in my life a long period of Family Clan living. It never got boring . . . Let's seize the day of recognizing our Common Goal and see how much it transforms for us.

Our Common Goal as an Intrinsic Given

Q. How can you say there is just one world view everyone should hold? . . . That will never happen.

A. *I* am not saying we have a common aspiration or Common Goal, nor am I saying "should." Our Common Goal is a given . . . . The fact that we each want "to love, be loved and be productive" is a basic intrinsic fact in the fundamental nature of human beings . . . Of course what we bump into every day and have to take into account, is the reality of people who are not loving . . . They perpetrate hideous violence, sex abuse, financial crimes, whatever, as has been said. But these people, as Erikson's and Bradshaw's work points out, have become hateful and encrusted in non-loving behavior out of their own emotionally deprived childhoods, and sometimes just from desperate adult situations where there is no real Oneness of Mind, or awareness of our Common Goal.

Politics

Q. I recognize the validity of your realization that we all do have—initially at least—until it gets knocked out of us — a Common Goal, in that we all want "to love, be loved, and be productive" . . .   But let's be realistic here . . .   A basic condition of life is that we have to compete for food, clothing, shelter, be we primitive man in the wilds, or on Wall Street . . .   My question is: how can we subscribe to 4-Loves loving, and yet compete for our basic needs, or for political office, or to be a member of Congress where Republicans battle Democrats daily to *win* — to get control — to put their own ideas across?

A. There is no question but that both our Economy and our Politics can be, and are used as a battleground for winning instead of cooperating. Winning is fine in sports and games set up for that purpose . . .   Winning in sports and games is fun for the players (we hope), and entertainment for others.

But in the bigger game of Life itself, when our major priority *is* to compete, we learn over and over that by not cooperating, especially in our Economics and Politics, we cause untold pain in stress, pace, failure, and loss of time . . . There is a current view which holds that we've had a divided government for the last 3 decades, in that the Democrats and Republicans fight on every issue from Roe vs. Wade, to judicial Supreme Court hearings. It was said that the reason such issues get so much focus on television is because our nation hasn't resolved these big issues yet . . . so we gnaw at them and thrash them about on television.

Might not the answer to the extreme polarization of such issues be for our political parties to seek *together*, using the Conflict Resolution Process to find joint, non-partisan solutions? We must keep discussions and debate passionate and vibrant, but if the goal is to resolve the issues rather than win versus the Other, the whole tenor of the situation changes.

Politicians, in order to keep their jobs, do want to win votes, but it is my bet that a politician who is big enough to see the issues, and take positions on how they can be resolved for the good of the whole, for everyone, *will* win politically . . . Sometimes it seems as though our government, instead of being of the people, by the people, and for the people, is instead a government of jobs, by jobs, and for jobs . . .

We need to reduce the insecurities surrounding jobs—perhaps by means of Re-training, Re-location Centers in the small Communities I have mentioned.

We need more Statesmen to choose from, fewer petty politicians . . . Again, it is my view that those who "see" what is missing for the good of All, and can offer solutions, will win politically. The 4-Loves perspective does work for both good and success. It works in earning a living or in politics. Its open, cooperative spirit even creates new jobs.

Abortion

Q. For example, how would you see the Supreme Court, or anyone, dealing with the abortion issue relative to 4-Loves loving?

A. It seems to me that the abortion groups, pro and anti, are not facing the real issue, due to not asking the real question . . . This is happening because neither side is asking, what is *loving* for the Mother, the Baby, and All, the Society? . . . If we think about what is loving for the Mother, can anyone but she and her doctor figure out what is best for her? If you ask, what is loving for the Baby? you have to think of the Baby's whole existence from conception through childhood. . . . Now that we know the terrible abuse, torture, living death most unwanted children go through, either at home or in foster homes, is the loving thing to allow such a baby to have an *unconscious* and peaceful release from such a life? . . . It seems to me when I try to stay in touch with my loving and concerned feelings, that early abortion is not murder, any more than a childhood and youth of torture, is murder . . . One is physical, the other psychological . . . One is unconscious and painless if properly done . . . The other, growing up abused, is conscious and exceedingly painful . . . And now that we know through Erikson's and Bradshaw's work, that to correct the emotional harm of such childhoods can be both hard and time consuming, *perhaps* it may be more loving to prevent such a life before it truly begins moving into *consciousness*. At least, both the pro and anti abortion points of view must be considered *relative to loving*, by the Mother and All of us.

I, for one, do not see death as the most unloving experience in life, either for the pre-born, the elderly, or painfully, terminally, ill . . . I see non-love, or a miserable *quality* of life as the most unloving experience. Did not Christ give up his own life for a chosen Quality of Life? When men go to war, are they not choosing death for themselves and others to preserve a Quality of Life?

So what can our Society do with such a difficult issue? No one is *for* abortion . . . Abortion, or the circumstances which bring an unwanted child into the world, are both undesirable. Would the most loving thing for our Society to do be to give freedom from attack to those already burdened mothers (and fathers, when there is one) and allow *them* to make this decision?

Perhaps the role of our Society, instead of fighting over a law, should be to set about overcoming the *root* causes of so many unwanted pregnancies, which are lost-ness, loneliness, and meaninglessness. We can do this by building responsible Fathers, Mothers, Families, Small Schools, small Communities with loving economic, political, and inspirational Systems such as we have been talking about . . . If we get busy with that, perhaps the need for so many abortions would fade away . . . The *issue* of abortion, however, will always be with us, and it seems to me that as a Society, we ultimately have to decide between giving loving freedom to the individual in this predicament, or making a rigid law that ignores what is loving for those individuals caught in this very human dilemma . . .

In my view, 4-Loves loving would at least change our focus and help us to get on with Community rebuilding as the most loving way to go for Mothers, Babies, and All . . .

Your view of what is loving may be different from mine, and because we care about each other, we should keep on talking . . . But it seems to me that no law will help these two problems before us: abortion which is unwanted, or having unwanted children who will suffer . . . We need to work in love, with love, on this difficult issue, listening to each Mother and try to help *her* decide, in her own particular situation . . .

Community and Singles

Q. With all this focus on Families in Community Design, where do Singles come in?

A. What is loving for Singles? Singles are much freer than families to do as they please . . . If they want to live in a City Center and have a group of friends there, fine. A great many Singles, especially women, the divorced and widowed, would prefer to be part of a geographic Family Clan. In a Clan of Families or friends they are never as lonely as they would be without them. There should always be privacy in such a Clan, but Clan members should live within walking distance of one another. To be able to go out of one's house and walk to a close friend's or neighbor's house, or bump into them walking around, or shopping, is sort of fun . . . Telephone networks, or a few interest groups to attend, is all most Singles have today, and it is just not as basic or satisfying as a geographic Community—especially in times of need or sickness.

Poverty

Q. What are we ever going to do with our poor, who are stuck in the inner cities and who have fallen through the cracks of our non-working Community Design and Systems?

A. I would recommend a radical Community Program for the whole country . . . Cities should be divided into a City Center surrounded by small communities of no more than 2-300 people . . . None of us can relate to more people than that politically, or in any other way. These small Communities should be redivided into Neighborhoods, and then into Clan groupings. The schema of Columbia, Maryland, is based on the growth of a family and is emotionally sound, yet Columbia is not perfect . . . There are many, small details that got lost in the doing of it . . . It is however, an extraordinary first step towards what is needed. Our present cities and suburbs as they subdivide into meaningful Communities for not only our poor but whoever lives there, need to do away with enough buildings that each family can have a small piece of land . . . Being in touch with land is as important to well-being as small-scale living.

The poor who are now trapped in our inner cities need to take part in this rebuilding. If our Government and inspired developers, joined with the poor on this thinking, the poor could be like our Forefathers in their new Colonies: build their own Community, and sell their services to one another. Someone should make a study of how our early Colonies managed economically. Perhaps there are lessons there that could be used today. . .

Husband, Wife, Father, Mother Roles

Q. Men and women seem genuinely confused about their roles as mates and parents . . . How does 4-Loves loving speak to these roles?

A. Well, if we love God, our Creator, The Force, whatever name we choose for the Higher Power, surely He/She created man and woman to be sexually attracted to one another . . . This in turn led or leads to having children, and that event creates a basic family unit, what we call today the "nuclear family" . . . So we might say that if we love God, we therefore have respect and honor for His/Her basic family unit design . . .

Throughout history the family unit has tended to evolve into groups of families, clans, or tribes . . . Today this kind of cohesion, under the influence of rugged individualism and a fracturing Society, is breaking down and apart, and we have all kinds of family patterns and groupings . . . However the nuclear family unit *is* basic, and if we love and respect our Creator, ought we not consider that structure as primary? It is also what is most satisfactory to most people, especially to children. If we listen to our children, each child wants his or her own Mother and Father *together.* Divorce is a horror (though necessary in some cases), and makes everyone miserable.

Our Creator, however, loves each individual and would surely understand our Singles for whatever reason they happen to build their own unique life-style or family patterns, because our Creator is most caring of those of us who have the tough breaks and who don't have the good fortune to achieve this ideal basic unit . . . I feel loving God means we would hope for this ideal basic Family Unit, as well as for Family Clans for All. This having been said, what is the role of the man and woman in such a marriage if they love their Self and the Other?

There are so many factors that shape roles . . . . For the sake of brevity let me boil things down to say:

1. Each couple should recognize they have the freedom to determine their own unique roles with each other because every relationship and every marriage is unique and can be different . . . . This determination should be looked at seriously and worked out *mutually* . . . . Each couple should understand our Common Goal, 4-Loves loving, how to use the Conflict Resolution Process, and how and where they want to live . . .

2. Understanding that, they should then work out their financial budget.

3. They should then face the question of whether or not they want children and when they want them. They should both have a course in Parenting.

If that takes care of Loving God, Self, Other, and Others (their children), in loving All they should consider the population explosion . . . Couples who want more than two children should make bargains with other couples who don't want children, so that they in clear conscience may have four children . . . . and if they only have two children they could live in Family Clans . . . This way they will find they have many of the benefits of having more than two children . . .

Lastly, couples who are guided by 4-Loves Loving, benefit from a Planetary Spirit and an humble sense of humor about themselves . . .

If men who understand what this writing is all about could take hold and be—in addition to basic providers—also romantic lovers (a joy all women genuinely need), I wonder if that single effort on the men's part wouldn't be the glue that keeps things going? . . . Men by nature seem right for leadership in this role. Women are for the most part romantic responders . . . The man could have such fun verbalizing his appreciation and caring of his wife *every* day, and he could take this responsibility of seeing that the two of them have at least an evening alone together every week. With this kind of relating and communicating, most women *do* respond and are basically happy . . . The jobs and financial aspects of marriage are essential and need to be earnestly worked out, but a romantic relationship is extremely important, especially to women . . . and I believe for men too. Yet it is the primary pleasure that most men ignore and fail to give. Marriages can break for lack of this, when all else is good in the marriage . . . We learn more and more that love *expressed*, and good communication using the Conflict Resolution Process, work to bring about the best in marriages.

In Defense of Men — In Defense of Women

Q. Let me continue with a question or concern of my own . . . Why has the divorce rate in recent years risen so high?

A. It is my view that until as recently as the late 70s, we didn't have the openness and communication we now have on television, or between people . . . But once the new milieu of saying what we felt became prevalent, along with women demanding equal opportunity, a lot of honest differences emerged between men and women, which no one knew how to handle . . . This resulted in fights and arguments and hasty bolting from marriages . . . The new honesty and openness was good, the too-quick bolting wasn't.

Now, however, having played through that new-found freedom of the 70s and 80s a bit, I sense we are entering a new era, one where the disaster of divorce and the importance of the family are coming back into focus . . . Concomitant with this evolution, we have the newly emerging Conflict Resolution Process, by means of which conflicts *can* be resolved and two people can come to understand one another. Couples must learn this Process and keep building towards their Common Goal of wanting each one to feel loved and be productive.

In defense of men, I want to say that I see us now in a period of transition . . . Men for thousands of years have been hunters and providers and warriors . . . By one ritual or another, they have been trained to be brave, and not to cry . . . No wonder it is hard for men to step into the role women now want them in, that of being emotionally sharing husbands and nurturing fathers. Even to-day our men are raised for tough competitiveness in business, professional life, sports, and yes, still war or defense . . . It is hard for men emotionally to wear both hats at once, though with this new understanding of what the new male roles require, their lives can now become more fulfilling.

In defense of women, I want to say women have long been the nurturers of children, as well as home providers for their men . . . Not all women even today want full time careers. Many would be happy to be in their historic role, if the men were emotionally and verbally the husbands and fathers they need . . .   Almost all women need some part-time vocational life, and if they could focus on family affairs and raising their children as their primary task each woman could find her own special path which would fulfill her various talents . . . When children are young, women do need more adult companionship and to satisfy this, some form of adult group sharing is essential for their well being . . . But after the youngest child is in school, women can more easily start part-time careers . . . A husband and wife, using the Conflict Resolution Process, can and must work out all these tugs and pulls . . . The major problem for most women is that their husbands let them down as communicative husbands, fathers, or providers . . . Therefore, with the feminist push for rights still abroad, many women compensate for that lack by taking on far more than they can handle . . . However, few women *want* to, unless they *have* to . . . Men and women do come from very different historic roles.

I remember when I was about 13 years old, standing on a bed and hurling a pillow at a high-boy across my room because I was just awakening to the fact I couldn't have a career and children too, and that men could. For several more years, I wanted to be a boy, an "impossible" I resolved by deciding to be a tomboy . . . The only real resolve, however, is when a woman is made happy and fulfilled for being a wife and mother, along with whatever part-time interests she can manage.

Again, in defense of women, I want to say to men that when you have daughters you will look at the burdens and needs of women with different eyes . . . ranging from menstruation to the very hard task of childbirth and long years of twenty-four hours a day nurturing. Child bearing and rearing must become just as much a vocation and honor as that of any man's.

Life is tough and demanding for both men and women . . . Let's have more compassion for one another and lower this destructive divorce rate. With the new insights we now have let's help each other love each other and be a joyous and productive team.

There are of course all kinds of special problems in marriages I have left out, such problems as alcoholism, wounded inner-child problems, marriages for the wrong reason etc . . . We desperately need to educate our early high-schoolers in:

Picking a Mate

The Nature of Marriage

Parenting

Conflict Resolution (If they have not already studied it. Many schools are already teaching it.)

Femicide

Q. As a woman I like your warm embracing view of life and your view of how we should relate to one another . . . There is a new term "femicide" which means "power-over" that I read about in a newsletter* . . . It points out how many women suffer the subtle uses of "power-over," and "less than" from men . . . ranging from daily manipulation to rape . . . How can we help men work more mutually with women?

A. As I pointed out earlier, men have been hunters, providers and warriors for thousands of years and women have been nurturers . . . I believe women are coming into their own in the 90s. This terrible unkindness and unfairness of men towards women is being recognized by many male doctors, counselors, and ministers; the younger generation of men are beginning to want a different role. The macho "power-over" image is passing . . . The only way we can help men is by pointing out to them this unkindness and unfairness, and by raising our sons to be aware that a "power-over" treatment of women, as against a relationship of mutual respect, is a corruption of power—one that only immature bullies or cowards would use.

Women, however, are capable of "manicide," which means the manipulation of men in ways that go beyond asking for mutuality in discussion and sharing.

Again, let us be loving of one another, we men and women, as we sincerely try to work out what is fair and kind for each of us.

*"The Feminist Paradigm and Conflict Resolution" by Ginger Ross Breggin and Peter R. Breggin, M.D., *ICAR Newsletter*, Spring 1992, vol. 5, no. 1, pp.1-6.

Temptation

Q. In view of all you suggest about marriage, what should couples do when either one of them experiences a serious temptation to another person?

A. That can happen even when a marriage is a good one and it is difficult . . . It causes genuine pain and violent headaches. I think the best antidotes are:

1. Remember your Love of God. You don't want to offend your Creator, *or* hurt your wife/husband, whichever it is . . .

2. Remember your Love of All . . . If *everyone* responded to temptation, what a mess we'd have . . .

3. Keep your sense of humor . . . I had a friend who once said: "I don't know what all this hurrah about temptation is . . . I never go out to dinner I'm not tempted." . . . He said that and laughed, but he meant despite temptation we are not meant to act on it . . . I agree with him . . .
If you have the unfortunate experience of having a serious temptation away from your home and family, get it out in the open by talking to a therapist, or a friend you can trust . . . Talking about it will help keep you from acting on it . . . Even tell your wife or husband if you can. Talk about it over and over, together, because whichever one of you is going through it, it just may happen to the Other one at

another time . . . But don't get in clandestine affairs . . . Two can play that game and it is a terrible game . . . For God's sake, stop before you act and get help, especially if you have children . . . If you and your mate can't develop through the years together, a marriage that is joy for both of you, maybe after the children grow up you can talk it over, and *mutually* decide to break it up. However, breaking up is no fun ever . . .

Temptation is tough . . . I don't minimize it. Try everything, rather than give in . . . Perhaps if you focus on being a good romantic mate, it will help see you through. View temptation as a normal experience that passes, and remember those people who have had the strength to resist it, are so glad later. They always wonder why they ever became so overwhelmed . . .

Homosexuality

Q. How does 4-Loves loving look at homosexuality?

A. Whew! This is a toughie because it is not yet known for sure whether or not there is a genetic or biologic basis for this activity, or whether it is somehow learned-behavior from the way in which we grow up . . . In the Sept. 9, 1991 issue of *Time* magazine the cover article was on this subject, and it indicated that despite much research, there is yet no clear proof from which we can be sure.

In my own effort to be loving of homosexuals, and to ask the 4-Loves question, I have come up with the following thoughts:

Since there is no known clear cause of this activity, we must each relate to each homosexual person we know with love, kindness, and interested listening . . . In the tangled, complex web of the unknowns surrounding this issue, each and All of us must conduct our Selves with a 4-Loves attitude and feeling . . . As time goes by, surely more knowledge will unfold . . . In the meantime we can contribute to that knowledge by lovingly listening to those homosexuals who are close to us . . . *Why* do they feel what they do, and *what* do they think caused their feelings? So few people dig deeply enough to understand themselves or Others.

I know so little in this area . . . I am eager to learn more . . . I can only say that I know so many, many lonely women of all ages that I wish men would not kill themselves off in wars or abandon us in any other way that denies us mutual love, family fulfillment, and fun.

Multi-ethnic Homogeneity

Q. You mentioned the two things in human relating where we have to accept the fact we inevitably will hurt others, namely, when we pick a mate, and when we choose our close friends . . . . It seems to me there is an inexorable drive towards homogenizing, integrating all races . . .   Does this drive come out of those hurts, out of what people feel are injustices, when according to you they are inevitable? And do we really want to homogenize the whole human race, or do we want to allow voluntary segregating for the well being of a Family Clan, as well as for protection of our racial and cultural differences?

A. Beautiful question and hard to answer. It seems to me that if we try to be as loving as we can be of each different race, we want to allow and encourage equal opportunity for education and vocational growth, no matter what. But at the same time, if a group of Asians or East Indians or Scandinavians, or Native Indians, or Blacks, whomever, want to live near one another in Family Clans, shouldn't we encourage that too? . . .   We have seen the value of Families, and Family or Friends' Clans, and I have recommended we build our Communities in ways that encourage small enclaves of Families or Friends, within a Community . . .   It has been my experience that some people *want* to live in small racially-mixed enclaves, and others do not . . .   Why can't we allow both instead of forcing anything? . . .   What matters most, as I think most will agree, is that each person has an opportunity for equal education and an equal chance to rise vocationally . . . .

There are other inborn unfairnesses we all have to accept other than choice of mate and friends, unfairnesses such as musical and art gifts or talents, dexterous use of hands talents, gift of good looks, athletic talents, and on and on . . .   Life is not fair in its distribution of inborn gifts and talents . . . and we need to accept these inequities. But we can all be loving and all have the joy of sharing in a fulfilling Family, job and Community life . . .

An International Children's Calendar published by AT & T for 1992 portrays five distinct racial and ethnic types on the cover: East Indian, Anglo-Saxon, Asian, Black, and Latin . . .   Perhaps we should add to that perspective a child of Mixed Heritage . . . . Usually the racially mixed take pride in their mixture and they want to be together. Why not recognize all types and let them mix or not mix as they choose. It will take all of us to help the world be loving . . .

Economics

Q. Why is our economic scenario represented to us by the going up or going down of the GNP, Dow Jones, etc? Why is it necessary for all enterprises to grow bigger and bigger in order to survive?

A. I honestly don't know . . . I am convinced, however, that of course the Economy should work for Man, not Man for the Economy . . . Again I suspect the wrong questions are being asked and studied . . . If the ground of wealth is human energy and human gifts, and there is so much work to be done in every Community and around the world, why can't we put these two ingredients together? . . . Somehow it seems to me we ought to be looking at what *human resources* there are in a given community, what *the needs* are in that community, and why the flow of money between these two doesn't give everyone jobs. Instead of reporting only on GNP, we should be reporting also on how Communities are working . . . How many people are there in a Community, and is there an adequate amount of money circulating there in relation to the population and its energies? . . . Too, there should be Retraining and Relocation Centers in each Community to see that people have work *in the Community* . . . Of course those people with the skills and the desire to go to into the National, or World Economy are free to go, but they have to fend for themselves. And if they fail they could return to work in their own or some other small Community, finding work through the Community Retraining and Relocation Center . . . It seems we need a two-level economy: the maintaining, not necessarily expanding economy of a small Community, managed by the Retraining/Relocation Center, as well as the growing, expanding National and

International Economy in which those who choose it can take part.

This may be of course a too simple answer, but if we ask about the welfare of *Communities* and report on how they are doing, instead of just national growth and bigness, we would surely be closer to having an economy that works for people . . . Jobs should come from meeting needs, not just from maximizing growth . . . We need a micro-cosmic economics for the small Communities as well as a macro-cosmic economy for the National and International communities. The big question is: Where is the leader who can inspire and direct us in this direction? . . . Where is the leader who can Nationally and Internationally *handle* the *immense* economy of this country? We need the Leader who can handle not only our macro-economics but can bring into being, and direct the management of, our small Communities' micro-economics . . . It is of course my view that if our economists would stop asking how we can compete better, and start asking instead, how we can create an economy that works for Communities of people, that we might get some refreshing vistas.

Building Communities is our much needed infrastructure, here and abroad. Building Communities, starting with the needs of the Individual, to Families, to Family Clans, to the total design of the Communities, including its shops and Systems, and connecting these Communities by rapid transit to City Centers, and spreading what we learn around the world just as we learn from other countries, is our greatest Economic and Social challenge . . . We probably don't need our present City, State, National demarcations so much as we need to look at bio-regions, their "carrying capacity"* as Communities, and connect them technologically by rapid transit and communications around the world.

*Carrying Capacity is a non-profit research center in Washington, D.C.

Disadvantaged Backgrounds

Q. Why is it that so many of our great and famous people so often come from deprived backgrounds? Does deprivation relate to success in any positive way?

A. I wouldn't say so . . . Many of our great and famous people come from supportive backgrounds too . . . Surely deprivation will either be overwhelming and handicap a child, or if the child is tough enough emotionally, deprivation may act as a spur, a driving force towards achieving success . . . . The danger is it may act as a driving force in the wrong direction. My question would be: why not give each child the joy and security a child deserves? Life is tough enough that just the living of it will take its toll . . . Not very many of us are tough enough to survive lack of love and support as children and young adults . . . We who have to deal with that burden find it adds to our adult struggle . . . Nothing upsets me as much as having to see a child or a young person suffer . . . Innocence abused by ignorance is a painful, painful scene to have to witness . . . Play it safe with the 4-Loves loving and the mutuality of the Conflict Resolution Process. I know from experience we and our children will have more fulfilling lives.

I once paraphrased the familiar bedtime prayer for my own children:

Now I lay me down to sleep,
I pray the Lord my soul to keep.
When in the morning light I wake,
Help me the path of love to take.

The Language of Love

Q. I heard someone say on TV: "Don't talk to me in those weasel words" . . . It seems to me that if you are always trying to be loving, guiding, evoking there is a danger of not being straight enough — not hitting someone with the honest truth! and the whole truth!

A. That is a danger . . . But be careful. Hardly any of us can take criticism easily . . . I heard a minister once say you have to have truth with love, and love with truth . . . Love without truth is flaccid . . . Truth without love is harsh . . . We always need to be both truthful and loving . . . Sometimes an introductory cushion will help to give an Other hard facts straight . . . Sometimes, if appropriate, the suggestion of using the Conflict Resolution Process may help . . . One's manner, tone of voice, and especially one's choice of words, will also make an enormous difference . . . In any event, we need to be both kind and honest and above all be *mutual,* loving the Other as well as our Self . . .

Pace

Q. I find that in the fast, fast pace I go in my business each day, plus some travelling, I have a hard time being loving to my family, except now and then. I bring home work I have to do, and all I want is for them to love *me* and make *me* feel good . . . I'm whipped, nothing much left over to give . . . 4-Loves loving makes sense and sounds great but, it takes too much time to even think about it. I don't find it helpful, except as an abstract guideline. If I ever had time to think about it, I'm sure it is a good guideline . . . I feel the same way about the Conflict Resolution Process . . . Takes more time than I've got . . . I just yell it out in the moment and somehow it all comes out in the wash, but I do feel more stressed than loving . . .

A. My heart goes out to you and all men and women feeling the pressure of life today . . . It is "awesome" as the kids say, and very depleting. What can be done about it?
There are some practical suggestions to try. Maybe one will help you, or if after hearing these ideas, maybe you'll come up with an original one of your own that will help you.

1. If it is possible to have "a decompression room" into which you can go for a half-hour on arriving home, maybe that will help . . . Then come out ready to relate to your family, geared down to family pace and needs . . . After the kids are in bed, do the work you need to, then spend a relaxing hour with your mate before bedtime.

2. Recognize there is no escape at home, and plan a full three day week-end trip

with your spouse and no one else, at least every other week-end.

3. I know a couple, both of whom are ministers, and when they realized their church work involved their nights *and* week-ends, this couple decided the only way to see each other, to talk alone, was to go out to breakfast every morning so no one knew where they were. There they shared their previous day and planned the one to come — read the paper and shared the world news . . . They thus felt in tune with one another and ready to go . . .   This couple had no children.

Children need a slow pace. They need a lot of calm as well as play, need a lot of hugging and rocking, and as they grow, they need developmental attention . . .   Small Communities related to Nature could help Families find a less frenetic pace. A fast pace is, in my view, antithetical to loving . . . It is antithetical to the deeper spiritual thinking we all need for taking stock of our Selves, and how we relate to Others. A fast pace can be exciting in the college and early single years, or as I've said, in the post-parental years, but while raising a family, well, it's often downright destructive.

Hypocrisy

Q. It is confusing to hear a lot of people talk about love and then watch them be anything but loving . . . Would you comment on that?

A. Hypocrisy. Saying one thing and doing another . . . This happens, I believe, because of the stages of growth we all go through when we are learning something new . . .

A person may hear an inspiring story or see something that causes them to get interested in love and loving, and they may then make a sincere reach towards being loving . . . But they are still caught in their old habits and patterns which prevail . . . The way we all learn is in three stages:

1. We get a glimpse of something new;

2. If we are drawn to that idea, we start learning about it and absorbing it;

3. We then internalize the idea, make it part of our thinking and being, our motive, our behavior. Only then is it integrated in us so that we start behaving congruently with the way we think or talk. As I've said before, one of the hard things in loving an Other or Others is that we are all on a Journey from non-love to love, and it is hard to know where a person is on his or her Journey. Therefore, we keep bumping into everything from superficiality to seeming hypocrisy and we are therefore lucky when we find people who are truly integrated, motivated, and mature in 4-Loves loving.

Population

Q. Whatever comes out of our quest towards fulfilling our Common Goal for each person, what can we do with the crisis in the world's population explosion? As you indicated before, too many people — more people than we can help to realize our Common Goal . . . . simply lowers the Quality of Life on all fronts, doesn't it?

A. Again, if we focus on human-scale Communities, *population must be controlled in any and every way it can be*, not only in this country but around the world . . . Information on the numbers a community can sustain, and education of us all in this is imperative!! . . . Each Community needs to deal with itself in this area . . . as well as having population experts informing us of the State, National and World scenes.

It constantly astonishes me that the population factor isn't the intrinsic base of any social or political plan, yet I never hear our politicians or community planners discuss it as a causal factor . . . How can they continue to ignore this basic factor which affects all Qualities of Life?

Judgment

Q. So often we hear "Judge not that you be not judged" . . .   This scares a lot of people and they won't speak up about the non-loving they see about them . . .   Would you comment on that?

A. The way I see judgment is that it means we are not to close off a relationship. Don't quit. Don't put someone down or close a door on them. It does not mean to not be discerning about a person or situation . . .   We must be that. Discernment in some dictionaries is a synonym for judgment and I find this very confusing . . .   We must discern but not judge . . .   We must discern in an effort to *help* someone, in order to be loving of them, not to put them down or close them off.

Family Clans

Q. This idea of Family Clans . . . which goes beyond nuclear families living independently is a new idea to me. Just why do you think Family Clans are such a good idea? . . . Seems too closed in to me. I like the idea of being around people I didn't grow up with. I like getting to know new people.

A. Perhaps you are not a candidate for a Family Clan Community, but prefer your own nuclear family to live in the country or a reasonably sized town, near a City Center . . . But if each of us asks, what is loving of God, me, my spouse, our children, and All, there are many of us who would choose a Family Clan Community. Each family must, of course, choose together whatever they want, and whatever their job or jobs dictate, but let me tell you some of the advantages of Family Clan living that many people don't even think about . . .

In having one's Family within walking distance of one another, yet each totally private, one gets those unexpected breaks I mentioned of bumping into each other, and having a spontaneous chat . . . or sitting under a tree together and talking in depth. To be able to talk spontaneously and peacefully, in depth, with eye to eye contact, is so much more fulfilling than just talking on the phone or having to plan a time to be together when there can be talk . . . So often when we do get together by plan, we forget all those *little* things we wanted to share at the moment, all those little nuances of thought that go through our heads and lead to deeper understanding. In planned gatherings our conversation is often forced . . . artificial.

By having these frequent and easy exchanges we tend to nourish a family's "oneness of mind" . . . We also eliminate for our elderly or ill, or singles for whatever reason, the loneliness they so often have to endure . . . In Family Clans we can build so much more easily a deep and caring relationship than we can in any other situation . . . The children benefit in that they have more than one set of parents whose views they can seek, and the children have automatic playmates until they are ready to be with special ones . . . To share a swimming pool or tennis court, if the family is so financially lucky is a natural family way of gathering . . . All of this is of course predicated on the fact that the families do get along relationally . . . Now that we have the Conflict Resolution Process, that should keep relationships open, healthy and joyous . . . It seems to me we all meet all the new people we can handle, in our schools and jobs, and that a healthy, happy Family Clan supplies a rewarding and enriching base from which to move out into the tough world outside . . .

No one is forced to participate in Family Clans, but with our new relational insights they could be a fulfilling joy that today many of us miss and yearn for . . .

It is important to note that Clans do not necessarily have to be made up of just family and blood relationships . . . They can also be made up of friends . . .

Family and Friends Clan Living has long been part of my thinking and is one of the pieces that got left out of Columbia, Maryland. Back in the 60's, I was working on such a plan called "Tooks Way." It consisted of nine residences with a central meeting facility . . . In that facility was a common kitchen and living dining area, a room for teen music and dancing a quiet sound-proof library where the elderly could gather . . . An exterior sketch is shown on the next page. In 1988, Kathryn McCamant and Charles Durrett introduced similar thinking in a book called *CoHousing.* Their plan also includes shop and work spaces.

A group in Maryland after reading the McCamant and Durrett book began the Frederick CoHousing Development Corporation . . . Either group could be helpful to anyone interested in this kind of thinking.

Central Meeting Facility of "Took's Way" — designed by Jean Lamuniére

Churches

Q. It seems to me that our Churches might well be Centers for Human Understanding, teaching healthy relating on all fronts, as well as teaching about a loving Creator and the resultant meaning and purpose in life . . .

A. Not only our Churches, but all our religious or humanist groups could take part in the 4-Loves kind of thinking . . . I agree that, besides teaching about a loving caring, God, as purpose and meaning in life, our religious institutions should teach the universal fact of our Common Goal and how that affects all our relationships . . . Love and loving and getting along with Others could be central and exciting in all religious and humanitarian groups, and even as each group retains special concerns and special ceremonies, all could recognize our Common Goal as a common unifying base.

Schools

Q. I hate what we so often hear today that our schools are not competitive in this world, that they should be more competitive. How does competitiveness in the world fit with 4-Loves loving?

A. It doesn't . . . If we love our children all around the world, and especially if we love our own children here in the United States, what has competitiveness got to do with educational goals? "Competitive" indicates we want to beat out in academic test scores the other nations of the world . . . We have to ask, "For what do we want to be competitive?" . . . To win a technological war so we can kill Others better or faster than they can kill us? . . . I have pointed out we have to be able to stand up to bullies, and we have to especially be able to stand up to aggressive national bullies, but we must not make that a prime focus of our Schools . . . If we give our children a loving atmosphere in which to learn, we will evoke their gifts . . . A joyous child using his gifts in a loving direction, will be far more productive and able to meet all future technological challenges than a child who is fearful, hurt, or ashamed, who is emotionally deprived, and emotionally polluted . . . With the use of his or her well developed gifts, well-adjusted adults can handle bullies when they need to . . . If we could spread the way to raise children all around the world, we might never have to go to war again . . .

I don't want you to feel I'm naive . . . I have lived through wars and depressions and I realize all the complications that beset the world, but I see so clearly what our values focus must be for emotional and relational well being. Think about how you, and I am thinking too, about how we can inspire our educators, develop our Communities and Schools in the way we see is needed. Let's get this world on the clearly visible Love track it must be on. Love has its own inherent standards and disciplines and we need the disciplines of Love, not constricting discipline for its own sake . . . If no one *initiated* anger or hurt-causing words or deeds to a child or an adult, we would reverse the world.

Schools are vital pieces of Community, and effective Schools and even our National well-being rest on the base of joyous, eager to learn, and fulfilled students.

Tastes and Values

Q. Why, if as you say, we all aspire deep down to love, have we so much demand for blatant sex, violence, and weird psycho shows on television and in our films?

A. This fact always baffled me until I began to realize that in a mass of people who were not made aware of our given Common Goal and who were therefore not inspired to pursue its fulfillment, we were bound to have many, many people who were lost from such a goal . . . . Each person comes here ignorant and needs to be inspired to reach that goal, else he/she is apt to fall into peer habits that are going in the opposite direction . . .

Either we recognize the goal deep inside ourselves and pursue it, or we don't . . . Either we work with Love, or we work against it . . . The only hope I see, as I've said over and over, is that we each and all must reduce our living Communities to human, manageable scale, and do all the things within those Communities that lift, not destroy, the feeling of higher minded Love and joy . . . We have to start with our infants, in well designed, small Communities, with small schools, small governments, and manageable economies, else we keep on breeding the "non-love side of life" . . . We don't have to be prigs. There are ways to give individuals the freedom to view the dark side, the non-love side of life without getting involved in it. In this generation enough films have been made of "the dark side" to last forever. . . Do you remember the Biblical story about the seven maidens who swept the devils out of the house, but didn't put anything new in? So what happened? Hundreds of more devils came in and took over the place . . .

Our Country, our Nation, and Community by Community needs to clean out its house and put emotionally and relationally healthy Systems in, or we never will win the battle of Love vs. non-Love . . .

Privacy Issue and Presidential Challenge

Q. How would 4-Loves loving handle the sexual exposures now facing our Presidential Candidates, and what do you see as what this country needs to look for in Presidential candidates?

A. This is plowing new territory for me. Let's take the first part first . . . What does 4-Loves loving say to our fairly recent inquiries into a candidates faithfulness to his wife? . . . In loving our Creator, we know He/She is always lifting us to the highest thoughts of Love . . . So if a candidate has cheated on his mate it could indicate a weakness in the candidate's character . . . It seems fair to ask: if a candidate cheats in one area, might he not do the same elsewhere?

If we are loving of the candidate, however, we have to look at the fact that we live in a period of transition. Once we accepted such matters as private, but now due to the new technological fluidity of the media, we accept looking at this area as "of our times." In the past we hardly knew anything about the private lives of our candidates. But we now know that most of our Presidents had affairs even while in office. With the exception of Jimmy Carter and Ronald Reagan, and now President Bush, a significant number of the others seem to have been to some degree unfaithful to their wives. So I see this transition in values as a healthy evolving of our marital standards to a more inspired level . . .

Also, now that women have become more outspoken, they are not going to let this issue be a one way game. If one can play it so can two . . . So on a practical as well as an inspired basis, duplicity in marriage is out . . . mutuality is in.

I have to say I like the way Bill and Hilary Clinton have been honest in sharing this issue with the American people. They have said that their marriage had been in trouble, but now they have forgiven one another and worked out their issues . . . What more can we ask from them? Nothing, if that all proves to be true.

As to the second point of your question, what should we be looking for in a Presidential candidate? I presume this was tied to the moral character issue . . . Surely we should look for impeccable morals: honesty, integrity, and dependability . . . But surely we must be looking also for that leader who can analyze our National problems and lead us out of them . . . All those problems we listed in the opening chapter on page 12 are obviously symptoms of something deeper that is wrong with our Country, and I hope we have addressed that "something deeper" in trying to point out our need to recognize our Common Goal, and our need for re-building all our Cities and Communities and their Systems with that Common Goal in mind.

Therefore, I would like to see a President who could lead the Governors and Mayors of this nation in the ways necessary to accomplish that kind of Planetary Vision, along with the practical re-building of our Communities in the ways we have discussed. No one man can accomplish this alone, but one such Leader could voice the challenge and begin to get us going. Perhaps we need two Presidents, one in charge of International Affairs and the macro-economics, and one in charge of the National and micro-economic affairs. Or if we had better stick to one President, we need to create a new Cabinet Post. Whatever, we would thereby be setting a model for the other countries of the world who now need to rebuild their own Communities and infrastructure . . . God bless him or her, wherever such a leader may be, and may they emerge soon.

Communicide

Q. Previously you addressed the term "femicide" which made me think of another possible new word . . . how about "communicide," meaning the behavior of someone who refuses to communicate, to use the Conflict Resolution Process in an open, sincere way searching for new solutions?

A. I think that would be an excellent new word, because there is now a new ethic involved here . . . we *must* communicate or we cannot relate . . . Broken relations due to *not knowing how to relate* is the core problem we must all face in the years ahead . . . Misunderstanding and broken relationships are at the heart of most of our domestic problems, as well as international conflicts.

World View

Q. Is it your view that if we can educate people to understand our Common Goal, to love with 4-Loves, embrace the Conflict Resolution Process, know the benefits of Balloon Brainstorming, and accept the Erikson and Bradshaw insights for getting to know and heal our "wounded-inner-child," that we might truly begin to win the battle for inner calm and peace? Do you believe we could then begin to relate to each other in a positive, loving manner, and start building a whole new world of vital Communities and City Centers?

A. That is my conviction . . . that must be our direction. It is a Clear Call . . . . Thank you for summarizing it so beautifully. Just don't forget, *your* life will be synthesized and integrated by following the Thread of your own Love feeling, balanced always by 4-Loves thinking . . . I believe that people who are aware of our Common Goal, and who are willing to express it as their motive as well as ask if it is the motive that others are concerned with, will build a prevailing milieu, a consensus that will eventually take over.

We have come to learn about environmental and chemical pollution . . . My hope is that this writing will help us learn about what I call relational pollution — a pollution of the heart and spirit, how to discuss it *mutually*, and what we need do about it—what we must do about it or be doomed to an unloving world.

To sum up, let us realize we make dozens of decisions everyday. May this writing have indicated for you the excitement and challenges of applying this view as the essence of our being . . . and in tough times remember this quote:

"I believe in the sun, even when it is not shining;
I believe in love, even when I feel it not;
I believe in God even when he is silent."

—Words found on the wall of a cellar
in Cologne, Germany after World War II.

APPENDIX

The Conflict Resolution Process

    The Conflict Resolution Process, depending on where and with whom it is used, can incur many steps, but in its simplest, most skeletal form it consists of 3 basic steps:

    1st *Listen!* . . . Listen to whatever another person says to you. Look that other person in the eye and give full concentration to what they are saying. (With small children, kneel down at their level so you can look them in the eye.)

2nd Make that other person *feel heard*. We need to do this in words that make clear to the other person that we have truly understood what they are saying . . . Do not just parrot them. Do this until the other says: "Yes, that is what I am saying. That is what I mean" . . .

The other person must then listen to your response and make you feel heard and understood . . . At this point, with two people understanding one another, bristles go down and they are ready to search for solutions that resolve the issue for both people.

3rd *Find win/win solutions*. This requires either a blackboard, or a large pad . . . The two people must then try to think of solutions that win for *both* of them, not just one of them, *both* of them. Herein lies the magic. When two people understanding their issue or conflict, come up with possible solutions that win for *both* of them, all kinds of new insights and answers emerge that in a locked-horns approach would never surface.

Put the win-win solutions of each person on the black-board or pad, and then both should participate in deciding which one or ones would be acceptable to both . . . If the first four or five ideas are not satisfactory to both, then based on what you are learning about each other's needs, try a new set of solutions until you find one . . . This process works!

Occasionally, if a solution cannot be found, you may have to agree to disagree — to suspend resolution awaiting light. However, even this can be done with understanding . . . accomplished amicably.

Dr. James Laue[2] says:

"A conflict is resolved . . . compared to terminated, settled, set aside, compromised . . . when the parties involved voluntarily and jointly develope an agreement which they believe meets their needs, improves their relationship, gives opportunities for action, upholds their values, and which they feel so good about they would never want to repudiate later."

[2]Dr. James Laue, Lynch Professor at the Institue of Conflict Analysis and Resolution at George Mason University, is internationally known as a mediator, trainer, and educator.

The 8 Ages of Man — Eric Erikson

Newborn
    Trust vs mistrust - fear of abandonment.

Toddler
    Autonomy - will of own vs shame and doubt.

Child (young)
    Initiative vs. guilt - "I am a bad, creepy child and I hate myself.
(Issue of trust vs. mistrust of self and other comes up at every step.)

Child (older)
    Competence vs. inferiority.

Youth
    Identity of unique self <u>vs.</u> confusion and not knowing who you really are.
    To find self must take chances.

Young Adult
    Intimacy, learning how to share self with another vs. Loneliness and isolation.

Middle Adult

Caring, creating, parenting, generativity vs. stagnation.

Old Age

All comes together in integrity—we develop a creative symphony of life vs. despair.

This produces a capacity to accept even death.

Scientist Sees A Revolution If Child Raising Were Sane

Los Angeles, May 1 (AP) — "The World could be transformed in one generation," says a psychiatrist, "if all parents would practice what we now know about raising children.

"There will be an unlimited future for mankind when this begins to happen," believes Dr. Charles W. Wahl, associate professor of psychiatry at the University of California at Los Angeles.

Dr. Wahl, one of the speakers in a U.C.L.**A.** series on "The Human Agenda — Biological Prospects and Human Values," said:

"Personal maturity and the capacity to love and work are primarily developed not through sociologic factors directly but through a loving and secure relationship within the biological family.

"Throughout all of history this most essential knowledge has been scientifically neglected and the raising of children left to 'common sense' and to folkways.

"In the past 50 years we have come to know, however, what needs to be done to raise a child to become a reasonably happy adult.

"Children need approval, security and challenge. These are simple things but they make a monumental difference in the child and later in the adult."

Dr. Wahl said many parents "seem to want to make their children go through the same hell they did in growing up." This is understandable, he said, but completely wrong.

"If interpersonal relations are going to improve - and I believe they are improving - the change must take place within the family," Dr. Wahl said.

Importance of Small Schools

Commentary:

Excerpt from Griscom Morgan's response to Esther Patterson's letter which appeared in the *Community Service Newsletter* (P.O. 243, Yellow Springs, Ohio 45387), January/February, 1988.

I am glad you are interested in the small school challenge. It is far more important than most people can imagine. The Carnegie Foundation was leading in the fight against small schools two generations ago but today it is out front for the small schools against the big. Studies have shown that small schools are less expensive for the same performance — or better. The record of performance of children from states with small schools (though far poorer economically) is well ahead of the wealthy states with large schools. The well-being of teachers and closeness of teachers to students and parents is much higher in the small schools than in the large schools. On paper, it can be argued that providing lots of specialists and expensive services would make far better education. But that is not the world for young children, any more than a big factory would be.

Basic Design Schema for New Towns and Old Cities

Small-scale Communities made up of Neighborhoods and Villages, with:

Privacy for each home—but within walking distance of one's own Clan,

Pathways for children to walk or ride bikes to school without crossing streets—or where possible, for children to ride ponies to school,

Public outdoor gathering, shopping and work places—neighborhood pubs, lots of them*,

Mixed generations

Open green spaces . . . with a deliberate wide band of green defining a Community, so dwellers feel a sense of physical definition,

Retraining, Relocation Centers within a Community Economy,

Rapid transit to a City Center and with access to a Center for Human Understanding, a "Pavilion of Life"

*London has 8,000 neighborhood pubs

ACKNOWLEDGMENTS

Key Influences and Helpers

Readings in Socrates, Plato, and Aristotle
Jesus' Teachings
Readings in and Life of Robert Browning
The Partnership Marriages of the Brownings and Pierre and Marie Currie
Harry Emerson Fosdick and all his writings and secondary references

Guthrie Speers — Presbyterian/Ecumenical Minister

Gordon and Mary Cosby; Betty O'Connor—Ecumenical Church of the
  Saviour in Washington, D.C.

Being married to a developer and raising our 3 children

Experiencing and participating in the planning of the new town of
  Columbia, Maryland

Serving on the Board of the National Peace Foundation

Landrum Bolling — Past President of Earlham College, Past President of the
  Lilly Foundation, and Mid-East promoter of peace

I. Shortess Yeaworth — World's Fair Pavilion Producer

Friends, books, and articles along the way

Editor — Thomas F. Monteleone

Publisher — Borderlands Press

Typists — Anna Schaffer & Delene Carlee